# Animals of North America
# AMERICAN BLACK BEARS

by Tyler Omoth

FOCUS
READERS

# www.northstareditions.com

Copyright © 2017 by North Star Editions, Lake Elmo, MN 55042. All rights reserved. No part of this book may be reproduced or utilized in any form or by any means without written permission from the publisher.

Produced for North Star Editions by Red Line Editorial.

Photographs ©: Sorin Colac/Shutterstock Images, cover, 1; Lynn_Bystrom/iStockphoto, 4–5; Red Line Editorial, 6; Tom Reichner/Shutterstock Images, 8; Jimmy Napp Photos/Shutterstock Images, 10–11; Don Mammoser/Shutterstock Images, 12; mikeledray/Shutterstock Images, 14, 29; tjwvandongen/iStockphoto, 16–17; NaturesMomentsuk/Shutterstock Images, 19; Frank Leung/iStockphoto, 20–21; Design Pics/Thinkstock, 22–23, 27 (top); troutnut/iStockphoto, 24, 27 (bottom right); Jerry Sharp/Shutterstock Images, 27 (bottom left)

**ISBN**
978-1-63517-030-6 (hardcover)
978-1-63517-086-3 (paperback)
978-1-63517-189-1 (ebook pdf)
978-1-63517-139-6 (hosted ebook)

**Library of Congress Control Number: 2016951025**

Printed in the United States of America
Mankato, MN
November, 2016

## About the Author

Tyler Omoth is the author of more than two dozen books for children. He loves going to sporting events and taking in the sun at the beach. Omoth lives in sunny Brandon, Florida, with his wife, Mary.

# TABLE OF CONTENTS

**CHAPTER 1**

## Roaming Wild  5

**CHAPTER 2**

## Built for Survival  11

**CHAPTER 3**

## Lone Foragers  17

THAT'S AMAZING!

## Hibernation  20

**CHAPTER 4**

## Black Bear Cubs  23

Focus on American Black Bears • 28
Glossary • 30
To Learn More • 31
Index • 32

# ROAMING WILD

Wherever there are forests in northern North America, there is a good chance American black bears are close by. American black bears live in much of Canada and the northern United States.

**American black bears are North America's most common kind of bear.**

Pacific
Ocean

North
America

Atlantic
Ocean

where American
black bears live

N
W  E
S

**American black bears roam wild in the northern areas of North America.**

They also live in warmer areas such as California, Florida, and northern Mexico. Sometimes, they are even found close to cities.

A forest is an ideal **habitat** for black bears for several reasons. American black bears are **omnivores**. Forests provide plenty of food that bears eat, such as berries and nuts. The trees also provide protection.

**FUN FACT**

American black bears make different sounds. A sharp, blowing sound indicates fear, while gentle grunting sounds often mean they are content.

 **Black bears are excellent climbers.**

Black bears flee to the trees and climb when threatened.

American black bears have very few **predators**. But sometimes

American black bears look similar to grizzly bears but tend to be darker and smaller in size.

grizzly bears roam the same areas. Grizzly bears are larger and stronger. They also have bigger claws and will attack American black bears. The American black bear, unlike the grizzly, can climb trees to escape to safety.

# CHAPTER 2

# BUILT FOR SURVIVAL

American black bears have small eyes, round ears, and short tails. With muscular bodies, they are very strong. They have long, narrow snouts. These are useful for finding food.

**Black bears stand approximately 3 feet (0.9 m) tall at the shoulders.**

 **Black bears can run, climb, and swim.**

They can reach into narrow openings with their snouts to get bugs and berries they like to eat.

Male black bears can weigh as much as 600 pounds (272 kg). Females are much smaller. They rarely weigh more than 200 pounds (91 kg).

**FUN FACT**

Black bears sometimes stand on their hind legs. They get their noses high up in the air to pick up the scent of food.

# PARTS OF AN AMERICAN BLACK BEAR

ears

snout

fur

claws

American black bears are agile.

They can swim very well and run

at speeds of nearly 25 miles per

hour (40 km/h). They also have

short claws. These claws help them climb trees.

Many American black bears have jet-black fur. But members of the **species** can have different colors. Some black bears are gray. Others are dark brown or cinnamon colored.

FUN FACT

The Kermode bear lives in the coastal regions of British Columbia, Canada. This kind of American black bear is actually white!

# CHAPTER 3

# LONE FORAGERS

American black bears are mostly **solitary** animals. They usually come together only in summer. That is when these bears mate.

Black bears spend some of their summer looking for a good den.

 Black bears spend much of their time foraging for food.

They spend the fall months eating as much as they can. The bears gain a lot of fat on their bodies. They will **hibernate** in their dens during the winter months. Caves or hollow trees can work as dens.

American black bears **forage** across large areas in search of food. Fruit, nuts, and grasses make up

FUN FACT

While hibernating, black bears only have to take a breath every 45 seconds.

 **A black bear lunges after a fish.**

most of their diet. They eat fish, young deer, and other animals when they can. Even garbage cans and dumps are occasional food sources.

# HIBERNATION

In some climates, food is scarce during the winter. American black bears have **adapted** a way to survive these conditions. When the colder weather hits, the bears hibernate. The bears spend most of the hibernation period sleeping. This allows them to use very little energy. Black bears can go as long as 100 days without eating, drinking, exercising, or going to the bathroom during hibernation. When spring arrives, the bears emerge from their dens.

A black bear's heart beats as few as eight times per minute during hibernation.

# CHAPTER 4

# BLACK BEAR CUBS

Females give birth during the winter months while in their dens. They usually have two cubs. Newborn cubs are blind and very small. They are completely helpless for the first few weeks.

 **At birth, each cub weighs less than 1 pound (0.5 kg).**

Two cubs closely follow their mother.

**It is possible for a mother bear to have as many as six cubs at one time.**

They drink their mother's milk until they are six to eight months old.

Cubs stay close by their mother's side until they are approximately two years old. At this point, they are ready to take care of themselves. Because the cubs stay with their mother so long, the mother only has a new litter every other year.

American black bears can live to be 30 years old in the wild. Their adaptability and ability to find food helps them live long lives.

**FUN FACT**

Most American black bear cubs are born with blue eyes that turn brown when they grow older.

# LIFE CYCLE OF AN AMERICAN BLACK BEAR

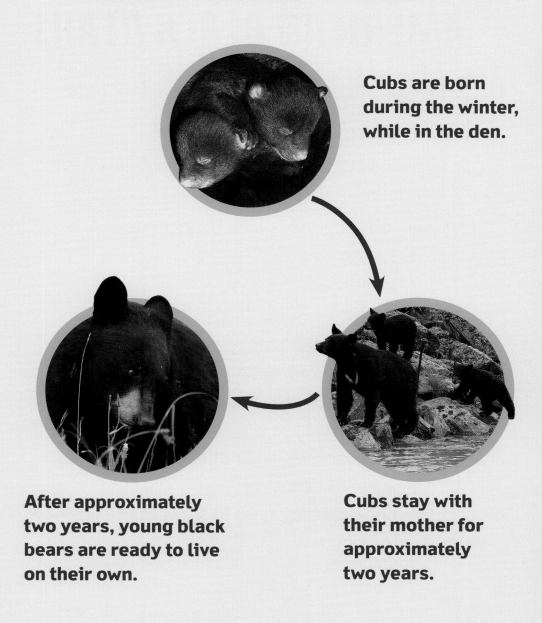

Cubs are born during the winter, while in the den.

Cubs stay with their mother for approximately two years.

After approximately two years, young black bears are ready to live on their own.

# FOCUS ON
# AMERICAN BLACK BEARS

*Write your answers on a separate piece of paper.*

**1.** Summarize Chapter 1 of this book.

**2.** Why do you think American black bears have few predators?

**3.** When do American black bears mate?
- **A.** spring
- **B.** summer
- **C.** winter

**4.** Why do American black bears eat so much during the fall months?
- **A.** because that is the only time they can forage
- **B.** because they will not eat while hibernating
- **C.** because they have to show their cubs how to hunt

**5.** What does agile mean in this book?

    **A.** able to move quickly and easily

    **B.** able to move slowly

    **C.** unable to move

American black bears are **agile**. They can swim very well and run at speeds of nearly 25 miles per hour (40 km/h).

**6.** What does **flee** mean in this book?

    **A.** walk

    **B.** swim

    **C.** run

The trees also provide protection. Black bears **flee** to the trees and climb when threatened.

*Answer key on page 32.*

# GLOSSARY

**adapted**
To have changed to better function in a certain place or situation.

**forage**
To search for something.

**habitat**
The type of place where plants or animals normally grow or live.

**hibernate**
To rest or sleep through the winter.

**omnivores**
Animals that eat both meat and plants to survive.

**predators**
Animals that kill and eat other animals.

**solitary**
Alone or without company.

**species**
A group of animals or plants that are similar.

# TO LEARN MORE

## BOOKS

Borgert-Spaniol, Megan. *Black Bears*. Minneapolis: Bellwether Media, 2015.

Jeffries, Joyce. *Black Bears*. New York: PowerKids Press, 2016.

Swinburne, Stephen R. *Black Bear: North America's Bear*. Honesdale, PA: Boyds Mills Press, 2014.

## NOTE TO EDUCATORS

Visit **www.focusreaders.com** to find lesson plans, activities, links, and other resources related to this title.

# INDEX

## C
claws, 9, 15
climb, 8, 9, 15
cubs, 23–27

## D
dens, 17, 18, 20, 23, 27

## F
forage, 18
forest, 5, 7

## H
hibernate, 18, 20

## M
mate, 17

## P
predators, 8

## R
run, 14

## S
snout, 11, 13

## T
tail, 11

**Answer Key: 1.** Answers will vary; **2.** Answers will vary; **3.** B; **4.** B; **5.** A; **6.** C